INSPIRATIONAL QUOTES
THE LORD SPOKE AND I WROTE

Written by

Julius R. Perkins

tGbG

ISBN: 978-1-7347692-0-3

Copyright Registration: 1-8714756871

This book is protected by the copyright laws of the United States of America. This book may not be copied or reprinted for commercial gain or profit. No part of this publication may be reproduced, distributed, or transmitted in any form or by any means or stored in a database or retrieval system without prior written permission of the Publisher.

Copyright ©2020 Julius Perkins

All rights reserved, including the right to reproduce this book or portion thereof in any form whatsoever.

Dear Moose,

How are you today? I pray all is well. I would like to say that after God, you are the best thing that ever happened to me. Thank you for loving me and showing what a godly husband is. May God forever bless and keep you, and that everything that your hands touch will prosper. Love you always and forever.

    Lil Moose

Date: 02/11/2017

Dedication

To my wife Mary P. whom I call "love" thank you for 42 years, 4 months and counting. You have stayed with me from "I do" to this present day. You are the reason I enjoy being married. You are my number 1 encourager and best friend. Through God's grace you have given me/us five daughters and twin sons. You support me and have prayed for me in our days of struggle. Now, you reap the years of prosperity. Thank you, thank you, thank you! I cannot say it enough. You still look amazing and I miss you more and more as we grow younger together. Always know that I received a great gift because of you being in my life.

LYA (Love You Always)

Your Husband,

Big Moose

Acknowledgements

To the Lord God who have me the wisdom, vision, and words to this book of quotes and poems. I couldn't do any of it without Him. Thank you, heavenly Father, for taking everything you put in my thoughts and putting it on paper. You even gave me the dates and times in my notes. To God be glory (tGbG) for it all.

To my five daughters and two sons whom I describe their character:

> Sheaneathea (daughter): Organizer, "Puts it together"
>
> Quionda (daughter): Planner, "Writes it down"
>
> Renee (daughter): Server, "The hands and feet"
>
> Marquita (daughter): Saver, "Saves the money"
>
> Elon (son): Educator, "Knowledge to wisdom"
>
> Tony (son): Teacher, "Trains the child"
>
> Jasmine (daughter): Social worker, "Fights for the elderly"

How do we see ourselves as parents?

> Mary Perkins (mom): Executive, "Makes sure things get done"
>
> Julius Perkins (dad): Visionary, "Sees it before, then call things into existence"

Alyassa Grimes Hooper – Thank you for your work in writing the manuscript.

Tony Perkins & Gena Gibbs– Thank you for your help in editing.

Introduction

Have you ever had a profound thought to come to your mind? A phrase, or wise saying and you did not write it down but wish you had. You then forgot about it or you wrote it down and lost it somewhere. Then years later you heard what was given to you in a song, on the radio, in a TV commercial or magazine ad. Well, through God's grace, He gave me many thoughts that I wrote down on small pieces of paper many years ago and some in this current year of 2019. While sitting at home on the bench in our bedroom, God gave me the thought of putting all those saying and quotes together in a book. Who would have thought that at 62 years young, God would have me writing my first book? The way I see it, if God inspired you to write it, then do it. I cannot wait to hear what happens as you read these poems and quotes. I know they will inspire you as they have inspired me. To God be Glory. (tGbG)

Julius Perkins

Contents

Chapter 1: Singles 1

Chapter 2: A Poem or Two 13

Chapter 3: Empowering Words 37

Chapter 4: When Two Become One 57

Chapter 5: The Truth Will Set You Free 79

Chapter 6: Think on This 119

Chapter 7: Words of the Spirit 155

Chapter 1: Singles

"Today, people may think that I am successful. I say, "No." The day I believed (God), I became successful."

--Julius R. Perkins

Single Lady T-Shirt

Single virtuous woman

Got wisdom like Solomon

Curves like a rainbow

I get mountains moved

Just by saying so

Now, what do you want?

Single Man T-Shirt

Single Man I

Created by I AM

Strength to conquer

Born to protect, I got a plan

Now, I ain't messing up; I for you

Selah

To the woman:

When a man tells you he loves you,

Listen with your ears.

Then ask him why,

And listen with your heart

Selah Selah

To the man:

When a woman says she likes you,

Pay attention.

When a woman says she loves you,

Don't take it for granted.

When a woman says no,

The law says no along with her.

If

If I don't vote and you do,

Then I stay sick while you get well.

If I don't vote and you do,

Then I get to know less while you get to know more.

If I don't vote and you do,

Then I don't live in the best house,

On the best street,

Drink the best water,

Or eat the best food.

If I don't vote and you do,

Then I can't write,

I can't read,

I stay in the same place while you move ahead.

Chapter 2: A Poem or Two

Mountaintop Love

Love is more than a feeling,

Yet, if you are human you can choose to feel love

Love brings us together; it does not divide.

True love conquers fear, builds bridges.

Love helps a stranger, treats him like a friend

Love pushes out the pride in us,

Humbles us, and is the source of true forgiveness.

With love all humanity rises together.

Without true (agape love) humanity falls

And fails even when it looks successful.

Thoughts

Thoughts come to me, saying you are too old for this.

A pain comes once in a while and says, you won't be able to finish this.

My own eyes look at me in the mirror of life and say,

Who do you know who looks like you who is doing this?

Yes, even my own money talks to me and says you can't pay for this.

Then I hear another voice saying, I am with you.

And another voice saying, don't quit.

And another voice saying, I am proud of you.

I have not changed my thoughts,

I just changed whom I listen to.

Mind Fight

In time to come
You will find out
That there is one person
And two spirits fighting for your mind,
you will in the beginning
Think for yourself.
Make your own decisions,
Ignore the help and take on the good
And the pain, somewhere in a quiet moment
you will see the two spirits that have been
Fighting for your mind all of your life even
Fighting for your bloodline, call it what you may
Good and evil, right and wrong, God and the Devil
Moral and Immoral...enough of this going back and forth in my head.
I need help, I want help, and I am going to start at the place in my mind
Where I found truth, love, peace, wisdom, and life everlasting.

Water

I am so transparent

You can see right through me.

I may not be the bread of life

but I am very close to it.

All that liveth need me to live.

Why, you can purchase me for pennies on a dollar.

In some places, I am priceless.

Men fought over me to own me

Yet I still go free.

You can find me on the Earth,

In the Earth,

In the air,

And even in the driest of places.

Yes, I am much like my Creator

Transparent, precious, everywhere.

Teenager

I know I got this, but I really don't.

I have a lot of energy, I learn fast, but I forget what's important.

I am carefree, no worries, except for my phone.

If you like me, or does my car look good?

I have heard from wisdom, but it was older

Even said that it loved me.

I know, I got this, but I really don't.

Weak Made Strong

A single snowflake so weak that

It melts in an infant's hand, but

When they stick together, they

Can roll down a mountain and overtake all

That is in their path.

Resilience

Look at me trickling down so slow

Looking weak you avoid me,

But I know you hear me dripping nonstop.

You surround me with sandbags, making cement into concrete.

I go through, I rise above

Dirt soaks me down; trees absorb me up

Yet somehow, someway, I keep pushing through

I keep rising, to the next obstacle that is in my way.

This isn't about the water you see,

This is about the water in me….

A Blind Man Sees A Woman

What is this coming toward me?

I see some similarities

But much different from mine.

I am distracted

My heart beats faster,

I am moved but in the same place.

It is so close now,

This beautiful creation

Touches me without lifting a hand

Somehow, I can feel communication

Yet no words were spoken.

Oh, no, it is passing me by and inching away.

Look at my hands shaking

Words in my mind

I want to speak

But my brain is in slow motion.

It is going to take me awhile to get back

To do what I was doing

Because I just saw

"Glory, intelligence, and beauty" going somewhere.

Listen and Learn

Doing wrong speaks to shame.

Shame speaks back to you

And tells you something is wrong.

When shame is confronted and lies,

Then guilt speaks to you.

When guilt won't tell the truth,

Then condemnation speaks to you.

Your conscious soul speaks to you

Over and over again

Even before you go to court.

Believe...the Shortest Route

Why when you open your eyes
All you see is what's in front of you.
You close your eyes and all you see is darkness.
Why is it that when others see you
They see a treasure of hidden talents,
And all you see is yourself
Normal and ordinary?
When do I see the
Diamond, the gold, the rubies,
The gifts of my hands?
When will I know?
What do I do?
How long do I wait?
I wonder what would happen
If I got rid of the why, when, what and how
And just believed.

The Bullet Catcher

When the time comes to stand up
Others said, not me
I am comfortable sitting down
We need money, someone said
You can't get mine
I don't have enough for my needs
We need more leaders
But one by one they bowed their head
And said, not me, you do it
I am not willing to take the criticism
I am not willing to lose my job
I am not going to make a little effort
Or the ultimate sacrifice
Then the unexpected happens
A voice said, "I will do it."

Chapter 3: Empowering Words

Breakfast, Lunch, Dinner

Walk in Love

Live in Peace

Eat the Word

Depart in Grace

You

When you see something you don't like,

First make sure that it isn't you,

Then go help change what you saw.

Wealth

Doing what you want to,

How you want to,

When you want to,

With whom you want to,

And the choice of not to do anything at all.

Alone

The further you get away from the flame,

the colder you become.

The further you get away from unconditional love,

The more prideful you become.

Maturity

May you be wiser now than you were a minute ago.

May you be more thankful now than your last complaint.

May you choose agape love above your own.

Speaking

"Words are very powerful once you put them out there. You are responsible for what comes back."

Together

You can do this!

I can do this!

We can do this!

Leader

I believe a person who is present,

Is more conscious

Than a person caught up in the moment.

For after the moment passes,

The person who is present

Knows what to do next.

Thank You

To the sanitation worker who picks up our garbage;
To the dishwasher in the back of the restaurant;
To the cook who works over the heat;
To the waitress who is underpaid;
To the truck driver who drives all night;
And to the 911 operator who is on alert all day;
To the policeman who protects;
And the firefighter who puts out the flames;
To the volunteer who is not known;
And to the surgeon who is known worldwide;
To the single mother who does it all;
And the father who did not leave;
To the nurse who does the work with all the technology;
And the missionary across the water who has none;
I have to stop now because my pen does not have enough ink.

Chapter 4: When Two Become One

My Wife

Behold, here she comes

The wind moves back and whispers

She walks softly, her arms, legs

And hips move in sync

She smiles and the sun covers its eyes

I tremble in anticipation

Waiting for her to speak

I just hope that I don't pass out

My Husband

This man loves me more

Than his own heartbeat; he supports me

Like the sky supports the clouds

He works harder than a bulldozer

Yet is gentle with his touch

Our kids call him Dad

I call him Lover

God calls him Friend

Twone

How do you make your marriage last?

Tell yourself in the best of times

I want to do this again,

So when the next day comes

You remember what you said.

Wife T-Shirt

"My husband does all of my plumbing work for free, honey."

Husband T-Shirt

"My wife still works magic: she makes me holler, and then puts me to sleep."

Priority

Work, work, work, work, work

It ain't about the money

It's about the honey

Love Is Priceless

You can't grow it out of the ground
You can't make it in a lab
As long as you share it with someone
You will never be poor.
You can't buy true love nor can you sell it
It can't be manufactured in a plant
You won't find it in a pill bottle.
Share as much of it as you can
Hold on to it and never let it go
Love will enable you to weather the storm

Love Trane

"Nothing can stop love wrapped up in a smile."

Agape

Love sees us through

Takes us through

Brings us out

Keeps us humble

Keeps us thankful

God's love,

It's a powerful gift.

Never let it go.

What Is the Measure of a Great Marriage?

"Longevity,"

No, you can be together a long time

And just tolerate each other

Saying, "I love you."

No, you can say it

Text it

Write it

And even sing it

And still not mean it.

Wealth, happiness, and family tradition

No, as good as all of these are,

I found that the measure of a great marriage is

Consistent truth, unconditional love, lifelong forgiveness,

Hard work, laughter, and peace in action from "I do"

Until your last breath.

Chapter 5: The Truth Will Set You Free

You and Me

Do you value me?

Do you know who I really am?

If I was hungry would you feed me?

If I was scared would you protect me?

Could I come to your cookout

Or live in your neighborhood?

Do you know that I have people who depend on me, love me, and call me friend?

Do you value me?

Backwards

"Wickedness is just knowledge going in the wrong direction."

Lukewarm

Why have the "Lord" in your life, if he's not going to be "Lord" over "ALL" OF YOUR LIFE…?

Where Are You?

No privilege

Some privilege

Thankful

More privilege

Too much privilege

More humility

More prideful

Too selfish

Too destructive

No privilege again

Circle of life….

Nothing and Nowhere

"Don't get yourself involved in nothing. It leads to nowhere."

Confused

Inconsistency is confusing,

God is not confusing.

If you don't know who He is,

Then you are confused.

Personal Selfish Pride

One of the greatest acts of selfishness

Is when one flawed human being

Tells another flawed human being

"I can't forgive you"

Why? Because the way I hurt

Is more important than the act you did

Struggles

"When my inability to operate in self-control yields to the temptation."

BAC .10%

It isn't the amount of alcohol in liquor

That causes the act of drunkenness,

But the amount that a person consumes

That causes the act of drunkenness.

Think

"A tragedy will humble you if you let it, or a tragedy can kill you if you don't."

Back and Forth

If you roll back anger

You will find fear.

If you roll back fear

You will find imperfect love.

Now you can stop here

And make a decision to turn around

And make the right move forward,

Or you can keep going

Until you roll back nothing.

Freedom

"When you are not worried about money then you can focus on what you need to do next."

Soul Tie Meets Addict

My thought is I am not going to do this anymore

It starts out good but always ends up in pain.

My thought is I am not going to call

Or answer the phone

But I do it again.

My thought is I won't get in the other car

Go to the other house

Or check into another hotel

Yet, I am back again.

My thought is I won't breathe smoke

Drink anything toxic, swallow pills

Or lose my paycheck at the table

Why am I back here again? I ask myself

My thought was not to be here.

Influence

Power is a powerful thing

If you give a person that is prideful power,

They become dangerous.

If you give a person that is humble power,

Then their wisdom becomes more noticeable

And helps their neighbors.

The Original and the Replacement

Sin has been replaced with the word "wrong,"

Holy Spirit has been replaced with the words "energy and feelings,"

Man and woman are being replaced with the words "they" or an "alphabet,"

Speak out has been replaced with the words "keep silent,"

Having sex is now replaced with the words "sleeping together,"

A lie has been replaced with the words "not true,"

We did it has been replaced with the words "I did it,"

Lord I can't do this without you has been replaced with the words "I did this by myself,"

After it all falls apart has been replaced with the words "I don't know what happened."

The Hungry and the Homeless

I saw someone in my trash

It was too big to be a cat

I saw someone else in the woods

It had two legs, stood upright

So I knew it wasn't a deer

I rode by, walked by, and even looked away

They looked like me

Of my same kind

I felt a little pain

Some sadness, but not enough to stop

After all, I don't know them

I don't live there

I am doing well

And if I keep going

The pain I feel will go away

And it did, but every time

I pass by that place

I lose something

A Tongue in the Wind

A mountain mover, a peacemaker
Even an encourager
Yet it can change quickly
Lightning fast and tear down that same mountain
Destroy decades of peace
It can heal and then cut into that which was healed
How can something so small, be so powerful?
It takes all your life to control it
Yet in a moment's notice it can become uncontrollable
As wild as a tornado
Destroying people, relationships
And even things made of wood, steel, and concrete
What genius would have thought that the world
Would have less destruction in it if sometimes
We simply kept our mouths closed

Disinfectant

Every scandal started with a thought

Every scandal spread started with a mouth to hear a conversation,

Every scandal stopped started with a thought of humility

Every scandal destroyed started with humility, truth, and repentance

Speaking out against the thought that started it all

Scales

I get on, I get off

A long time goes by

I get on, I get off again

My mind is not made up

My body follows my mind

Only when I see my health

More important than the disease

Then the scales will become my friend

Chapter 6: Think on This

Dirt

From the smallest twig to the redwood

I hold them together and lift them up

I give stability to those that walk

And foundation to the skyscraper

I separate the oceans from the rivers

And the lakes from the streams

How could the Golden Gate Bridge rise

Or Niagara Falls drop without me?

What's on top is expensive,

But the bottom is priceless?

Wise Up

"I wouldn't even have sense enough to be stupid if God withdrew His hand from me."

Doubt

"You have faith as long as the outcome is in your favor. You have fear when you don't know what's going to happen next."

Cash Walking In

"The customer is not always right, the customer is not always friendly, but the customer is always the customer."

Fraternal Twins

"Knowledge is knowing; wisdom is knowing how."

Truth

"You can tell a lie on the Truth, but you cannot make the Truth out of a lie."

Timoney

"When time saves you money, use the time.

When money saves you time, use the money."

Virtue

It takes wisdom to be right

It takes courage to be wrong

It takes humility to be both

Let's Talk

Written or spoken communication

Was thought to be just talking and writing

NO! Communication is understanding exactly

What is being said by the person who said it

The person who hears it, and the person who reads it

Think First, Speak Second

"Words are too important to waste. Speak wisely."

Be Quiet

"Don't talk while listening, just listen."

There Is and There Are

There is one word a person

Doesn't want to hear: "cancer"

There are at least two words a person

Doesn't want to admit to: pride and adultery

There are at least three words that are hard to say:

"I was wrong," "You were right,"

And "Please forgive me"

There is one name above all others: "Jesus"

There are two names that make one: husband and wife

There are three names that equal one: "Father, Son, and Holy Spirit"

Time for Sale

There is no such truth as:

Can I buy a little more time?

Time is so valuable

That even the richest of the rich

Can't buy it

The Question/The Answer

The question Does God exist?
While pondering on the simple profound things
I thought about the sweet potato being birthed in dirt,
Who gave it sugar,
The night owl perched high on a tree branch
Hears a tiny mouse walking in a hole
The evergreen stays green
And the little bee makes honey that doesn't spoil
The whale, geese, and butterfly
Go from one side of the Earth to the other
And don't need a map
You can even find water in the dry desert
And grass pushing up through a concrete driveway
And if you need more convincing
A microscopic sperm found a microscopic egg and made you
No Mother Nature or Father Time
Could do these simple, profound things
As for me the day I received salvation
And the countless times
I have received grace and mercy

The many times I have witnessed unconditional love

Toward humanity,

Yes, the Lord God does exist for me

For if He did not, all of creation would have destroyed itself

Hinges

"Little decisions behind closed doors lead to bigger decisions in the open."

Wise Counsel

"You can waste a lot of your own life giving wisdom to people who won't listen…stay wise."

GOD/CEO

Companies are profit driven,

Visions are God driven

Led by the Holy Spirit.

Chapter 7: Words of the Spirit

Growth Process

"Pray, watch, listen, learn. After that, pray, watch, listen, and learn some more."

Message Delivered

God has heard your prayers.

It's going to happen.

It's already happening.

I (God) cannot lie.

You have seen me do too much for you.

Do It

Pray the Word

Preach the Word

Practice the Word

I AM JESUS

I saw you before you were

I predestined you before you came

I gave you dreams, visions, and a plan

I gave you undeniable resistance to overcome it all

I fought for you, understood your pain because I felt it myself

I am known by many names;

Teacher, Master, Savior, Redeemer

But I would like to be your BFF (best friend forever)

The Anointed Holy Spirit

I feel you moving on me

I don't know when you control your timing

I feel at peace now

You make me much smarter than I am

Because you brought wisdom with you

I couldn't do this without you

Fear had a hold on me

I am not worried about that

Now I feel your power, you knew that

I needed that, too

My mouth spoke

I heard what was said but was amazed

Because I knew I didn't say it

I am in awe

You feel closer to me than my own skin

I am glad we are together

I don't want to leave your presence

The Name Jesus

Gave away more cars than Oprah

Has more followers than Facebook

Holds more money than the Federal Reserve

Rescued more people than the Red Cross

Healed more bodies than any vaccine

Traveled more miles than the frequent flyer

Faster than Usain Bolt

Stronger than Superman

Turned water into wine and walked on it, too

Did more changes than the Transformers

Created the apple before the iPhone

The name of Jesus is...

Unstoppable

All Powerful

And Everlasting.

Triplets

I would rather have favor than mercy.

Favor is receiving a blessing that I didn't earn.

Mercy is not getting a rebuke that I did deserve,

And grace is like a mediator;

It stands in between and decides

When I get favor or mercy.

About the Author

I was born in Greenville NC, the year of 1957. I met my wife in high school and married after we graduated in July 23, 1977. We have now been married over 42 years. We have five adult daughters (Sheaneathea, Quionda, Renee, Marquita, Jasmine) and two adult twin sons (Elon and Tony), one son in law Patrick Artis (Renee), one daughter in law Ariel Perkins (Tony), and two grandchildren (Toni and Cassidy Perkins). I am also the co-owner of our own homemade ice cream business call "Cravin Cravings" which was launched out 2 ½ years ago. I am an over the road truck driver for 22 years now.

I have a calling on my life to preach and teach the gospel in a way that is easy to understand. Plus, I enjoy providing marriage counseling to singles and couples. My wife and I attend Showers of Blessing Christian Church in Rocky Mount NC under the leadership of Pastor Dr. Bernard Grant.

Special honor to the many daughters and sons who have chosen me to be a mentor and/or father like figure in their lives. I will only mention a few of the many but know that I have love and respect for All of you. (Imani Brooks Wheeler, Sharon Smith, Kim Smith, Kesha Little, Mesha Featherston, Calvin Johnson, Tyrone Barnhill, Nicolette Peer).

www.ingramcontent.com/pod-product-compliance
Lightning Source LLC
Chambersburg PA
CBHW071345080526
44587CB00017B/2974